PRAISE FOR G.R.O.W.

This book is an absolute gift to the world. It's affirming, practical, grounding, and a timely resource for us all!
Mariel Buqué, Ph.D.
Psychologist & Generational Trauma Expert

As a creative, a perfectionist, and a perpetual over thinker, I am so grateful to have these tools that help me to engage my dream projects with love, ease, and affirmation! This productivity guide is perfect for folks like me who get overwhelmed easily, who sometimes feel like our goals are too big to achieve, who just need a little hand holding as we prepare action plans towards achieving our wildest dreams.
dr. reelaviolette botts-ward,
Author of mourning my inner[blackgirl]child

As an artist & innovator from Baltimore. I always had big ideas and dreams, some of which didn't even feel possible to achieve. Especially having self doubts that would affect my confidence, & self-expression.

This productivity guide is allowing me to take my goals one step at a time, while I'm discovering new things about myself and creativity, which takes the mountain of pressure & anxiety off my shoulders as I plan for a bodacious future!
John Tyler,
Emmy-Nominated Multi-Hyphenate Artist

Concentration is the ability to control your thoughts and organize your knowledge into a plan of action that is sound and workable.
Nothing was ever created by a human which was not first created in the imagination, through desire, then transformed into reality through concentration.

Napoleon Hill, The Law of Success

Concentration is one of the key currencies of today's world. That's where the most value is: in your ability to concentrate on your chief aim, one task at a time.

Joseph Rodrigues, YouTube Creator

G.R.O.W. PRODUCTIVITY GUIDE

100 SELF-PACED STRATEGIES

Acknowledgements

Sharayna Christmas

Mikea Hugley

The Paper Herald of Mount Vernon - Baltimore, MD, USA

───────────────────────────

G.R.O.W. Productivity Guide: 100 Self-Paced Strategies

Copyright © 2024

G.R.O.W. Formula & Graphic Design

Valenciá D. Clay-Bell

Print & Digital Publication

Fabian D. Bell

All rights reserved, including the right to reproduce this work

in any form whatsoever, without permission in writing from the publisher,

except for brief passages in connection with a review.

www.GrowCeryGarden.org

ISBN 978-0-578-94557-6

ISBN 979-8-218-14675-7

HOW TO USE THE FORMULA

G:  START WITH PROMPTS TO
get clear
& confident

R:  APPLY COGNITIVE TOOLS TO
read &
refocus

O:  ORGANIZE, PLAN, & EXECUTE
one task
at a time

W:  REFLECT ON YOUR PROGRESS
when finished,
create

G.R.O.W. Productivity Guide

CONTENTS

Fade the habit of procrastinating and amp up your productivity with this workbook featuring 100 strategies for self-determined success!

Instead of regular page numbers, we use a special code, like G9, R13, O6, W2, to find each way to grow!

It's like a game with 4 rounds:

Round 1: G

Round 2: R

Round 3: O

Round 4: W

The aim is to feel really good by engaging in or completing a task all by yourself, using prompts from G to W to help you.

Above each prompt, there is a grow-statement to plant positive thoughts in your conscious, before using the strategy.

G.R.O.W. Productivity Guide

GET CLEAR & CONFIDENT

G1: Describe Yourself
G2: Determination
G3: Goal-Setting
G4: Motivation
G5: Engagement
G6: Intention
G7: Purpose
G8: Abundance
G9: Ease
G10: Stillness
G11: Optimism
G12: Envisioning Celebration
G13: Peace
G14: Boundaries
G15: Read, Watch, Listen
G16: Priorities
G17: After-Journaling Ideas

G.R.O.W. Productivity Guide

READ & REFOCUS

R1: Productive Environment
R2: Reading Plan
R3: Just Start
R4: Start, Space, Start Over
R5: Progress Tally
R6: Study & Stretch
R7: Naming the Noise
R8: Tallying the Noise
R9: Eliminating the Noise
R10: Timelapse
R11: Daydream Monitor
R12: Stamina Graphing
R13: Academic Boredom
R14: Foldables
R15: Vision Board
R16: Personal Reading
R17: Share Your Learning

G.R.O.W. Productivity Guide

ONE TASK AT A TIME

O1: Executive Function Rank
O2: EF Task Checklist
O3: Bitesize Goals
O4: Task Calendar
O5: Organize, Breathe, Start
O6: Hourly Checklist
O7: Task-Specific Checklist
O8: Countdown Timer
O9: Brain-Break
O10: Alternative Starts
O11: Task Perseverance
O12: Self-Check-In
O13: 20/10 Hack
O14: Off-Task Impulses
O15: Self-Compassion List
O16: Timelapse Goal Reminder
O17: Working-Memory

G.R.O.W. Productivity Guide

WHEN FINISHED, CREATE

W1: After-Productivity Ideas
W2: Gratitude Tree
W3: All the Feels Wheel
W4: Dream Catcher
W5: Define Your Success
W6: Personal Progress
W7: Measure Your Success
W8: I Was, I Am
W9: Everything Sheds
W10: I See Myself As
W11: My New Name Means
W12: Framing Reflection
W13: Sensory Reflection
W14: Original Short Story
W15: Patterns and Lines
W16: Dots and Doodles
W17: Creativity Dump

G.R.O.W. Productivity Guide

DIRECTIONS

5 WAYS TO USE THIS GUIDE

1 Use the planning or zine templates on the following pages to customize how you complete G.R.O.W. strategies daily, weekly, or monthly

---

2 Try:
G prompts before productivity
R + O prompts during productivity
W prompts after productivity

---

3 Complete the prompts in this book, a digi-notebook, or paper journal

---

4 Use a board with sticky notes to make a visual, as you track your progress

---

5 Use the "off-task work space" as a blank journal for thoughts before, during, or after productivity

G.R.O.W. Productivity Guide

Date

Creative Goals

Daily | Weekly | Monthly
Productivity Checklist

G.R.O.W. Strategies

G: _____
R: _____
O: _____
W: _____

Reflect on 3 Words to Describe Your Growth

_____
_____
_____

share your growth @g.r.o.w.guide

G.R.O.W. Productivity Guide

MAKE YOUR OWN ZINE
FOLDING INSTRUCTIONS

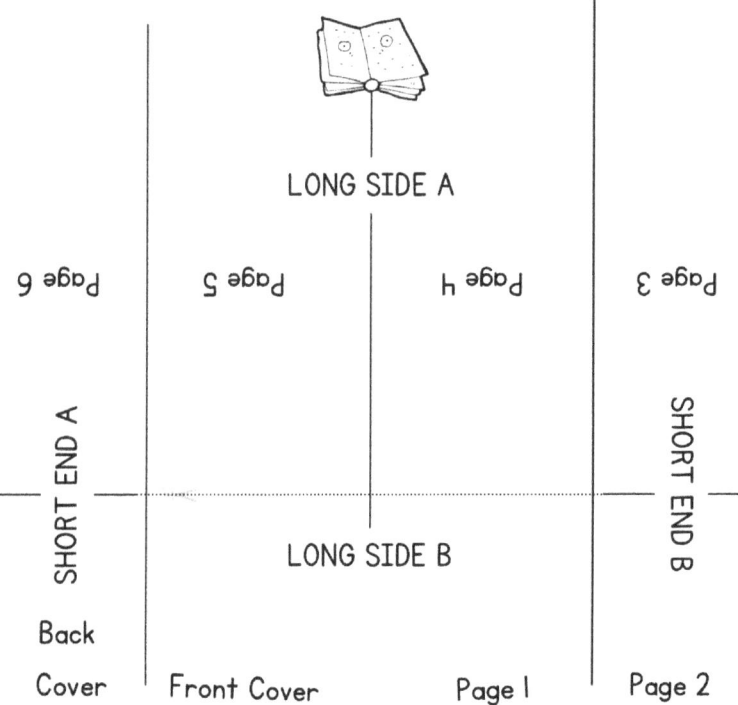

Step 1: Fold along all lines, ensuring a good crease.

Step 2: Fold the paper in half, aligning Shorts Ends 1 and 2, then cut along the dotted line segment only.

Step 3: Fold the paper in half lengthwise, aligning Long Sides A and B to reveal a diamond shape where the cut was made. Use the prompts in the template to design your zine.

G.R.O.W. Productivity Guide

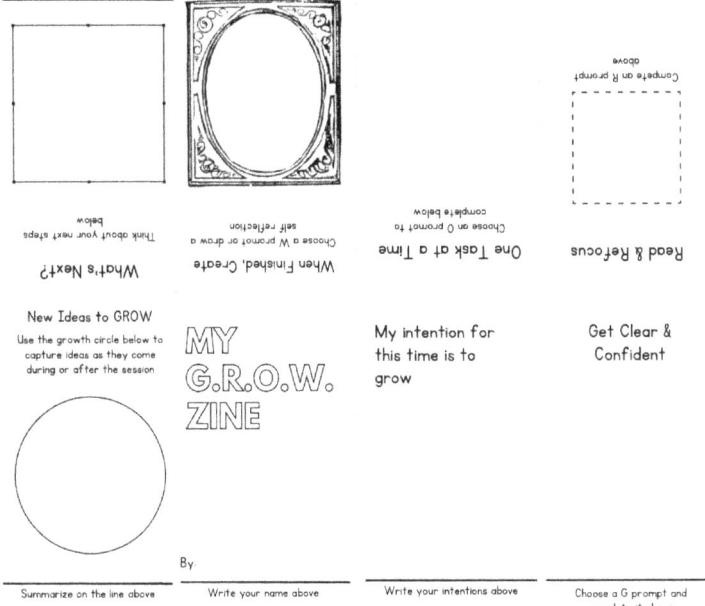

**USE A BLANK SHEET OF PAPER TO MAKE YOUR OWN ZINE
FOLLOW THE PROMPTS ABOVE OR CREATE YOUR OWN**

G.R.O.W. Productivity Guide

G.R.O.W. Productivity Guide

GET CLEAR & CONFIDENT

Graphic organizers and prompts to guide you before you start your productivity session.

G

Grow beyond your comfort zone
to unlock new levels of creativity

Grow above the noise by staying focused on your goals

extra thinking space

Grow through challenges to
emerge stronger and more resilient

Grow beyond limitations to
unleash your full potential

extra thinking space

Grow above distractions to
maintain peak productivity

What are 3 steps you
can take towards
your goals
for the work?

What are 3 ways
you can remind
yourself of
your goals?

Grow through setbacks with perseverance and determination

extra thinking space

Grow beyond expectations by exceeding your own standards

What is the **motivation** for your work? Do you have a personal connection?

G4

Grow above the competition by innovating and adapting

extra thinking space

Grow through failures as stepping stones to success

What keeps you fully **engaged** when your motivation seems to escape you?

Grow by innovating and adapting

extra thinking space

Grow above self-doubt with a
mindset of confidence and belief

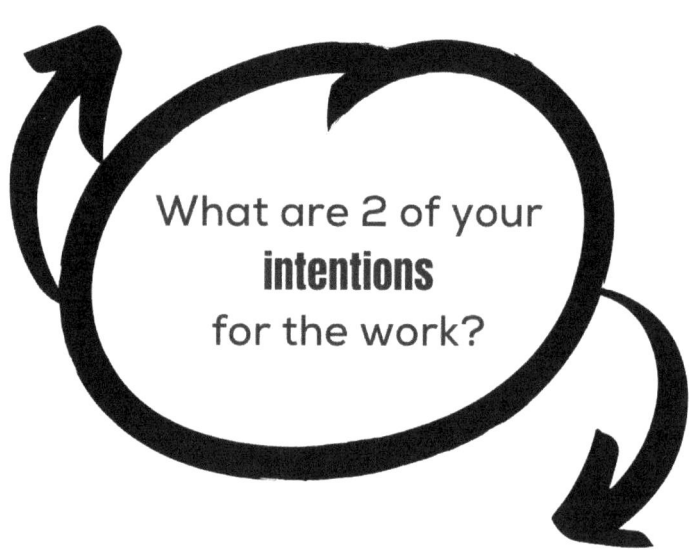

What are 2 of your **intentions** for the work?

Grow through feedback to continuously improve and evolve

extra thinking space

Grow beyond fears by embracing uncertainty and taking risks

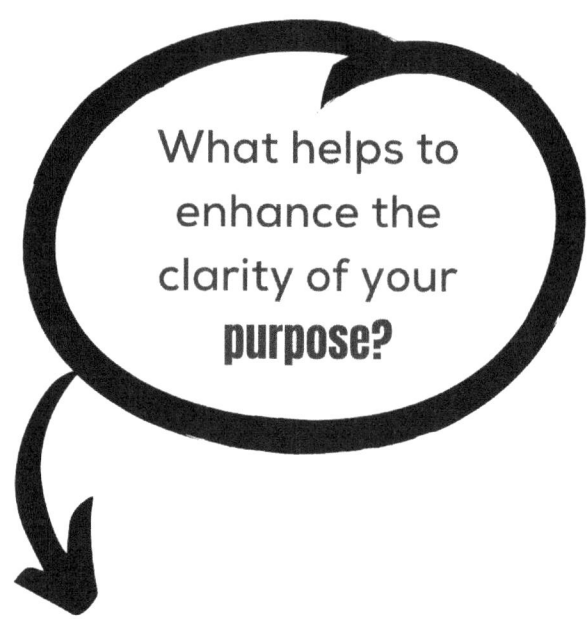

What helps to enhance the clarity of your **purpose?**

Grow above the crowd with a unique approach to problem-solving

extra thinking space

Grow through collaboration to leverage collective creativity

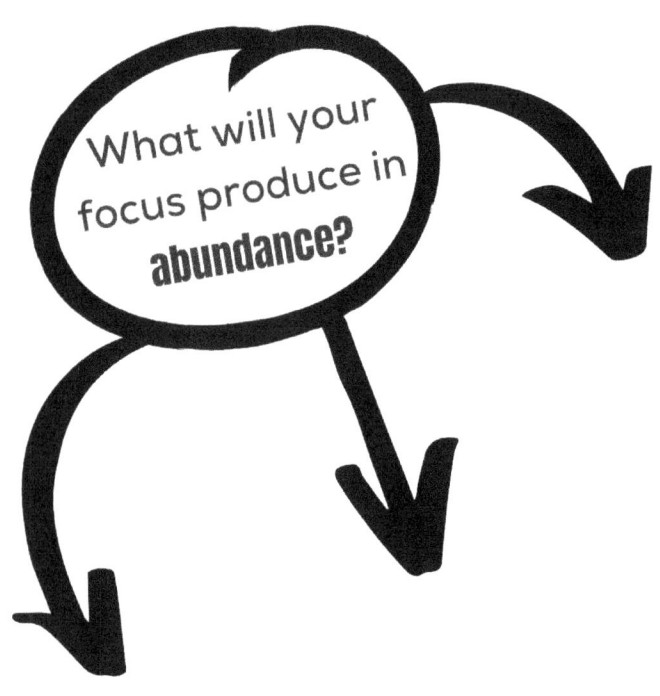

Grow with a unique approach to problem-solving

extra thinking space

Grow above distractions by
prioritizing focus and discipline

What do you need
to bring you
ease
as you produce
creative ideas
or start tasks?

Grow toward innovation

extra thinking space

Grow beyond limitations with a mindset of abundance and possibility

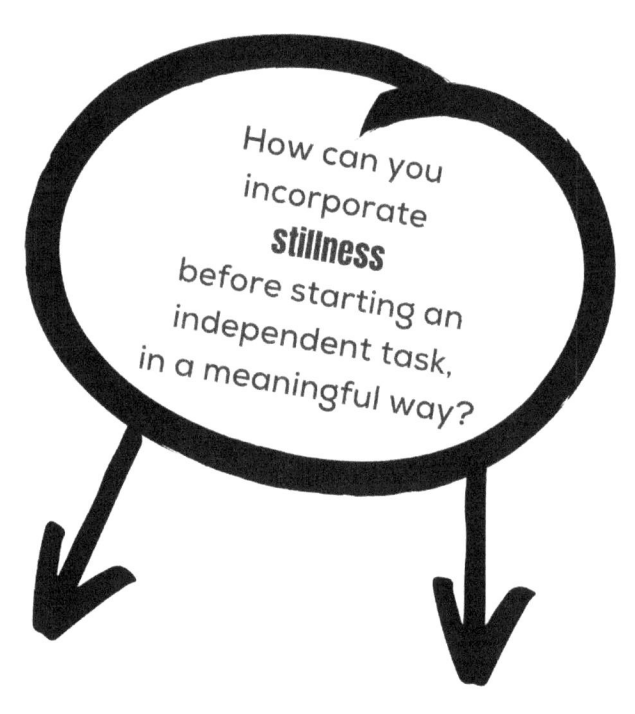

Grow above mediocrity by striving for excellence in everything you do

extra thinking space

Grow through discomfort to expand your comfort zone

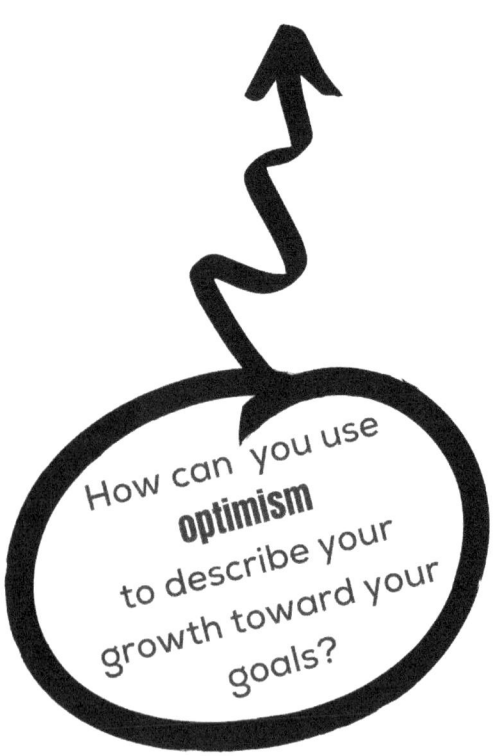

G11

Grow by striving for excellence in everything you do

extra thinking space

Grow above self-imposed barriers by challenging your own assumptions

Grow through reflection to gain
insights and self-awareness

extra thinking space

Grow beyond the status quo with a commitment to continuous improvement

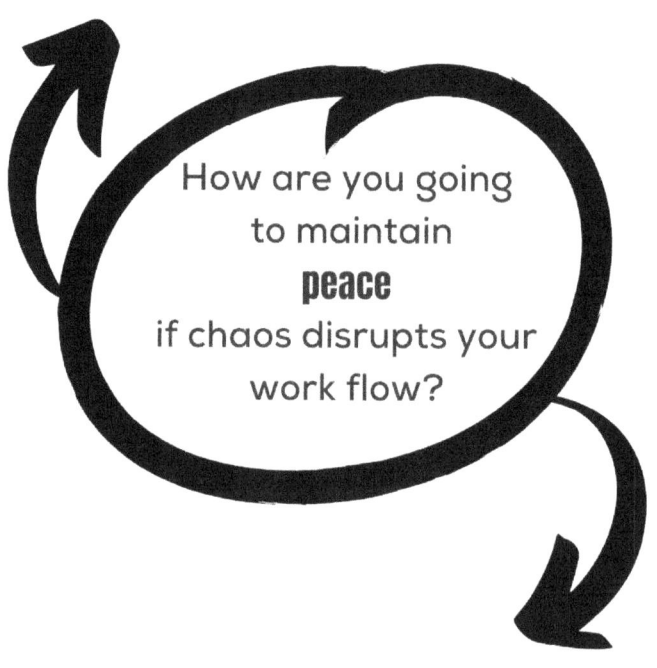

How are you going to maintain **peace** if chaos disrupts your work flow?

Grow through ongoing reflective journaling to gain self-awareness

extra thinking space

Grow through setbacks with grace and humility

How will you create **boundaries** to protect your time, space, and energy before starting a task?

Grow beyond conformity by embracing your unique strengths

extra thinking space

Grow above distractions by staying aligned with your priorities

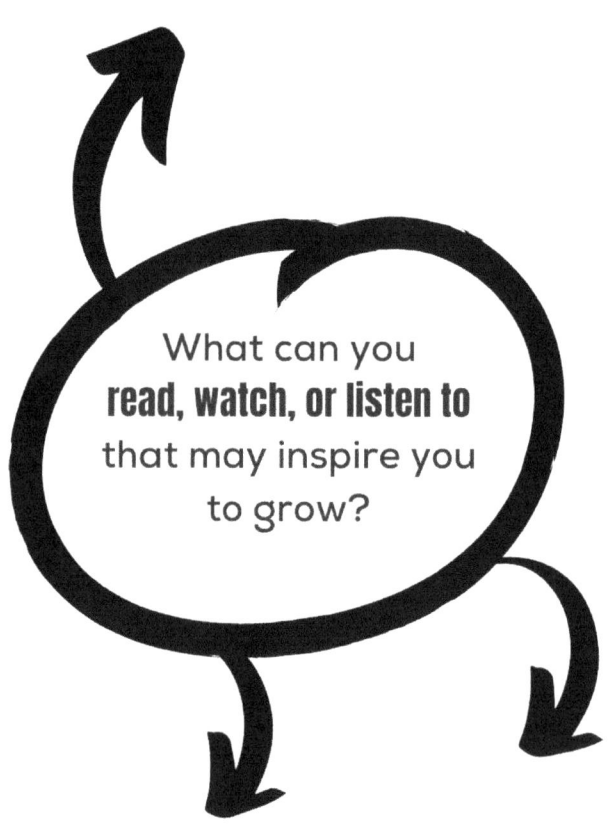

What can you **read, watch, or listen to** that may inspire you to grow?

Grow by embracing your unique strengths in unique ways

extra thinking space

Grow beyond obstacles with
creativity and resourcefulness

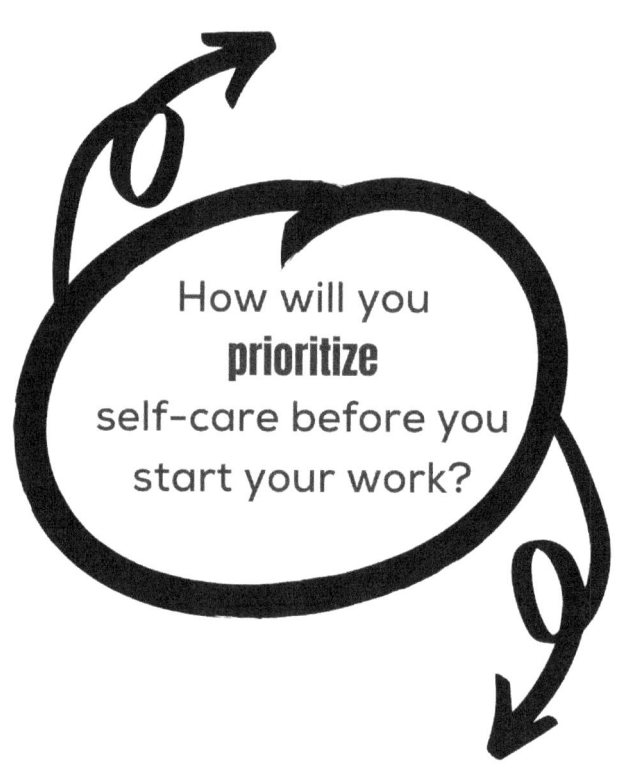

How will you **prioritize** self-care before you start your work?

Grow above self-limiting beliefs by expanding your mindset

extra thinking space

Grow through mistakes as opportunities for learning and growth

After Journaling Ideas

Set To-Do List
Stretch
Walk
Jog or Run
Full Body Work Out
Bike Ride
Hydrate
Meditate
Shower
Wash Face
Eat a Filling Meal
Read
Silent Drive
Listen to a Podcast or Music
Start a Small Task

Grow beyond your past achievements
by setting higher aspirations

extra thinking space

G.R.O.W. Productivity Guide

G.R.O.W. Productivity Guide

READ & REFOCUS

During-reading strategies to enhance the focus of your attention on the text.

R

Grow above the noise with clarity of purpose and vision

Ideas for Setting a Productive Environment

Organize Your Workspace
Set Your Ambiance
Play Hz Frequency Music
Set & Track 1 Goal
Visualize Your Success
Drink Lots of Water
Eat Nutritious Snacks
Use a Lumbar Pillow
Put a Plant on Your Desk
Set a Timer
Pre-Plan Guilt-Free Breaks
Remember Your Purpose

Grow beyond expectations by pushing the boundaries of what's possible

Grow above complacency by embracing a mindset of continuous growth

Plan Your Reading Out

Use a calendar to map out the page numbers you want to read in a text. Follow the calendar as a way to remind yourself to meet your reading goals.

If you miss a day(s) on your calendar, move them to another day. Keep working with your own reading schedule to determine the best days and times you are most productive while reading.

Grow through adversity with courage and perseverance

extra thinking space

Grow by being different and embracing your authenticity

Just Start

Start a timer and give yourself 15 minutes to just start. Try going for 3 rounds to get 45 minutes of productivity in. Use the final 15 minutes to take a break.

If you "just-start" and have trouble focusing on reading,
space out the reading.

Grow above distractions by prioritizing learning time for personal development

extra thinking space

Start, Space, Start Over

If you "just-start" and have trouble focusing on reading, space out the reading. Do something else for 15 minutes, then start over with your reading session.

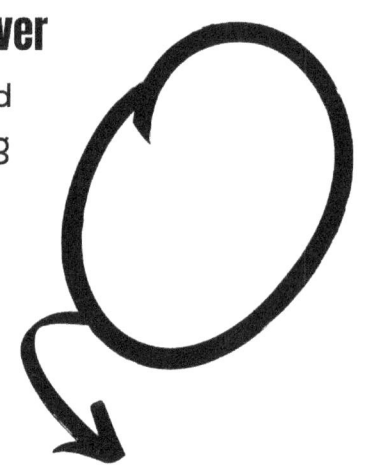

Grow beyond the confines of your own experiences through the power of storytelling

extra thinking space

Grow beyond resistance by embracing the discomfort of progress

Progress Tally

Use a timer to work in 20-30 minute productivity sessions. If you work through the session, without getting distracted, give yourself a tally. After you finish, count how many tally marks you have and create a goal to have more progress tally marks during your next session.

Grow beyond the limitations of your own
language by exploring literature in translation

extra thinking space

Grow above the distractions of social media by immersing yourself in the timeless art of reading

Study and Stretch

Set a timer and goal to be productive for a 20-30 minute interval.
After the interval, take a 10 minute stretch break. Next, reset your 20-30 minute timer, create a new goal, and complete your productivity session.

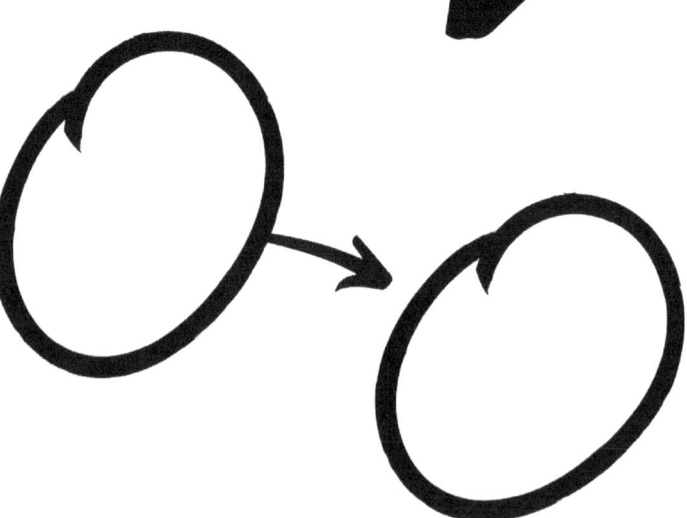

Grow through progress, not just through success, but also failure

Grow beyond setbacks by seeing them as opportunities for progress

Naming the Noise

What are you hearing in your mind as you are trying to focus? Track your thoughts with a focus wheel each time you notice a distractive thought. Title the wheel once it is complete.

For example: "Distractions of a Loving Heart" or "Fears About the Future" or "Regrets and Ruminations."

Grow through the pages of history and literature
that inform and shape our understanding

extra thinking space

Grow beyond the past by focusing on progress in the present

Tallying the Noise

During productivity, if you experience a distracting thought, use a tally mark to track the number of times they occur but push yourself to keep focusing on completing your goals beyond the distractions.

Grow creativity by exploring new mediums and techniques

extra thinking space

Grow concentration by practicing mindfulness and focus techniques

Eliminating the Noise

Develop a focus wheel of 3-4 empowering thoughts that may help you to redirect and eliminate mental noises during productivity sessions.

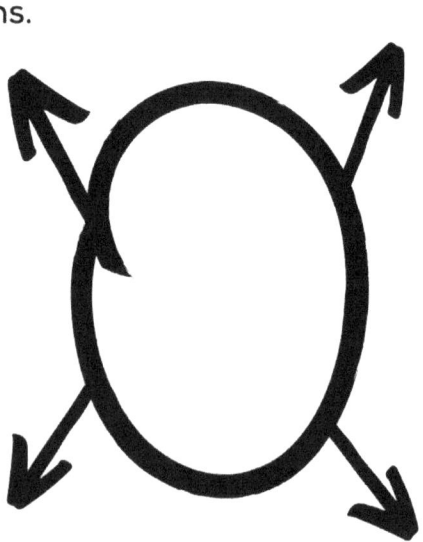

Grow beyond trauma by seeking support and healing resources

extra thinking space

Grow creativity by embracing failure
as a natural part of the process

Timelapse

For self-accountability, use the time-lapse feature of your camera to record yourself during productivity. When you are finished, share your progress using a private or public vlog on TikTok or Instagram reels.

Grow productivity by setting clear goals and priorities

extra thinking space

Grow concentration through regular meditation and mental exercises

Daydream Monitor

Whether negative or positive, if you find yourself daydreaming while working, take a break to make a focus wheel or draw your visions.

After analyzing your daydream, take 10 slow, deep breaths and restart your productivity session.

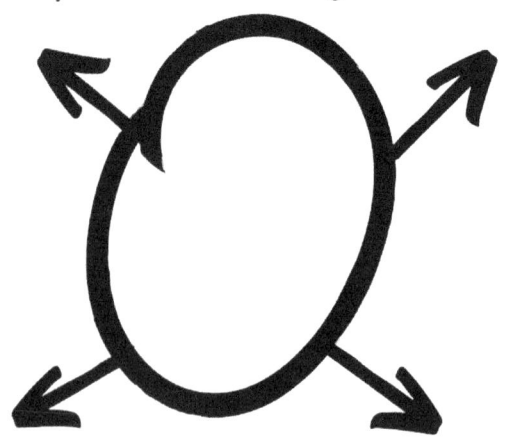

Grow beyond trauma by acknowledging and processing emotions

extra thinking space

Grow productivity by minimizing distractions and staying organized

Stamina Graphing

Set a goal to build your current page number count and/or minutes of time reading.

For instance, set a goal to read 20 pages in 30 minutes.

Create a line, dot, or bar graph of your progress. Add to the graph to show your progress toward your goals.

Grow understanding of neurodiversity
by listening to diverse perspectives

extra thinking space

Academic Boredom

If you find your reading assignments to be so boring that it is affecting your ability to understand what you read, try to make it more interesting by listening to the screen reader (check the accessibility settings on your electronic device) or try finding video versions of the readings online.

Use a note catcher to capture the gist from the audio or videos, then, go back to the text to see if you can understand what you are reading.

Grow concentration by limiting multitasking and focusing on one task at a time

extra thinking space

Grow creativity by exploring different genres and styles of expression

Foldables

Use index cards or make foldable paper cards for each new idea you learn during productivity.
Use the cards as a reminder of your progress. Recall the information on them, at least 3 times, before moving on. You may want to hang the cards or glue them into a journal in the form of a learning-journey scrapbook.

Grow productivity by delegating tasks
and asking for help when necessary

extra thinking space

Grow concentration by practicing gratitude and mindfulness in daily life

Vision Board

Make a focus wheel to categorize what you envision to be produced as a result of the work you are doing. Create a visual collage of the list by finding photos or words that encompass the list. If digital, make it your screen saver. If you use paper such as sticky notes, hang in your work space.

Grow beyond trauma by finding healthy outlets for self-expression and reflection

extra thinking space

Grow creativity by stepping outside of
your comfort zone and trying new things

Personal Reading

Choose a novel, periodical, or self-help book that has nothing to do with your tasks.
Either read 15 pages or read for 15 minutes.
While reading, escape the world of productivity and focus on the text.
After reading, be productive in your work for 20-30 minutes. Start personal reading again, during your next 15 minute break.

Grow productivity by setting boundaries and saying no to tasks that drain your energy

extra thinking space

Grow creativity by embracing curiosity and maintaining an open mind

Share Your Learning

If you find yourself getting distracted by the excitement or even the boredom of your work, develop a space
to teach others what you are learning, as you go.

Try creating a Twitter or blog/vlog that allows you to share keys you highlighted, study notes, an outline of main points,
or a dump of thoughts you have about the subject during your productivity sessions.

Grow productivity by setting boundaries and saying no to tasks that drain your energy

extra thinking space

G.R.O.W. Productivity Guide

G.R.O.W. Productivity Guide

ONE TASK AT A TIME

During-productivity strategies to enhance the focus of your attention on the task.

Grow concentration by practicing self-awareness and recognizing when focus is drifting

Number Your Executive Function Strengths & Areas for Growth from 1 to 12

Initiating a Task
Organizational Routines
Persistence
Impulse Control
Emotional Awareness
TIme Management
Working Memory
Sustained Attention
Planning and Preparation
Flexibility
Social Thinking
Metacognition

Grow beyond trauma by finding healthy ways to express yourself and process emotions

extra thinking space

Grow by embracing challenges as opportunities for growth

Make an Executive Function Checklist You Can Implement to Complete Your Task

- [ ] _____
- [ ] _____
- [ ] _____
- [ ] _____
- [ ] _____
- [ ] _____
- [ ] _____
- [ ] _____
- [ ] _____
- [ ] _____
- [ ] _____
- [ ] _____

Grow by prioritizing self-care and well-being to fuel your journey of growth

extra thinking space

Grow by seeking feedback and constructive criticism to refine your skills and abilities

03

Grow by celebrating progress, no matter how small, and staying focused on the journey ahead

extra thinking space

Grow by fostering a sense of curiosity and openness to new experiences and perspectives

04

Grow by practicing gratitude and finding joy in the present moment

extra thinking space

Grow by challenging limiting beliefs and reframing them into empowering affirmations

Grow by taking ownership of your choices and actions, and holding yourself accountable

extra thinking space

Grow by investing in personal and professional development through continuous learning

Use an Hourly Checklist to Plan Your Day

- ☐ 5:00 _____
- ☐ 6:00 _____
- ☐ 7:00 _____
- ☐ 8:00 _____
- ☐ 9:00 _____
- ☐ 10:00 _____
- ☐ 11:00 _____
- ☐ 12:00 _____
- ☐ 13:00 _____
- ☐ 14:00 _____
- ☐ 15:00 _____
- ☐ 16:00 _____
- ☐ 17:00 _____
- ☐ 18:00 _____
- ☐ 19:00 _____
- ☐ 20:00 _____
- ☐ 21:00 _____

Include your daily distracting tasks such as emails and social media to stay engaged and in flow.

Grow by cultivating resilience and bouncing back stronger from setbacks and failures

extra thinking space

Grow by focusing on solutions rather than dwelling on problems or obstacles

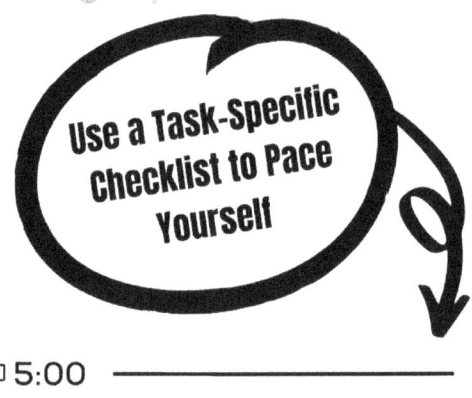
Use a Task-Specific Checklist to Pace Yourself

- ☐ 5:00 ———————
- ☐ 6:00 ———————
- ☐ 7:00 ———————
- ☐ 8:00 ———————
- ☐ 9:00 ———————
- ☐ 10:00 ———————
- ☐ 11:00 ———————
- ☐ 12:00 ———————
- ☐ 13:00 ———————
- ☐ 14:00 ———————
- ☐ 15:00 ———————
- ☐ 16:00 ———————
- ☐ 17:00 ———————
- ☐ 18:00 ———————
- ☐ 19:00 ———————
- ☐ 20:00 ———————
- ☐ 21:00 ———————

Grow by prioritizing your passions and pursuing activities that ignite your purpose

extra thinking space

Grow by staying committed to your goals, even when faced with challenges

Grow by finding inspiration in the success stories of others to motivate your journey

extra thinking space

Grow by taking intentional breaks to rest and recharge, nurturing your mind, body, and energy

Grow by cultivating a sense of purpose and aligning your actions with your aspirations

extra thinking space

Grow by embracing uncertainty and seeing it as an opportunity for adventure and growth

O10

Grow by practicing self-reflection and gaining insight into strengths

extra thinking space

Grow by being proactive and taking initiative to create the life you desire

Grow by practicing kindness towards yourself
and others, recognizing we are all on a journey

extra thinking space

Grow by challenging yourself to constantly push beyond your limits and expand your potential

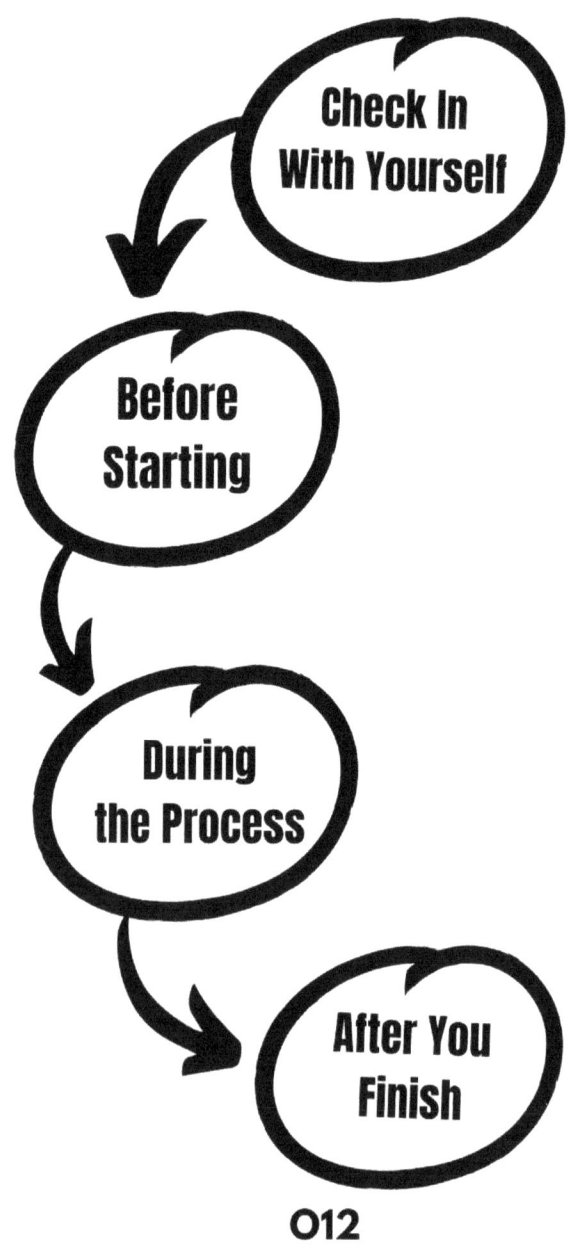

Grow by embracing discomfort as a sign of progress and pushing through resistance to reach new heights

extra thinking space

Grow by seizing the present, making the most of opportunities for growth and transformation

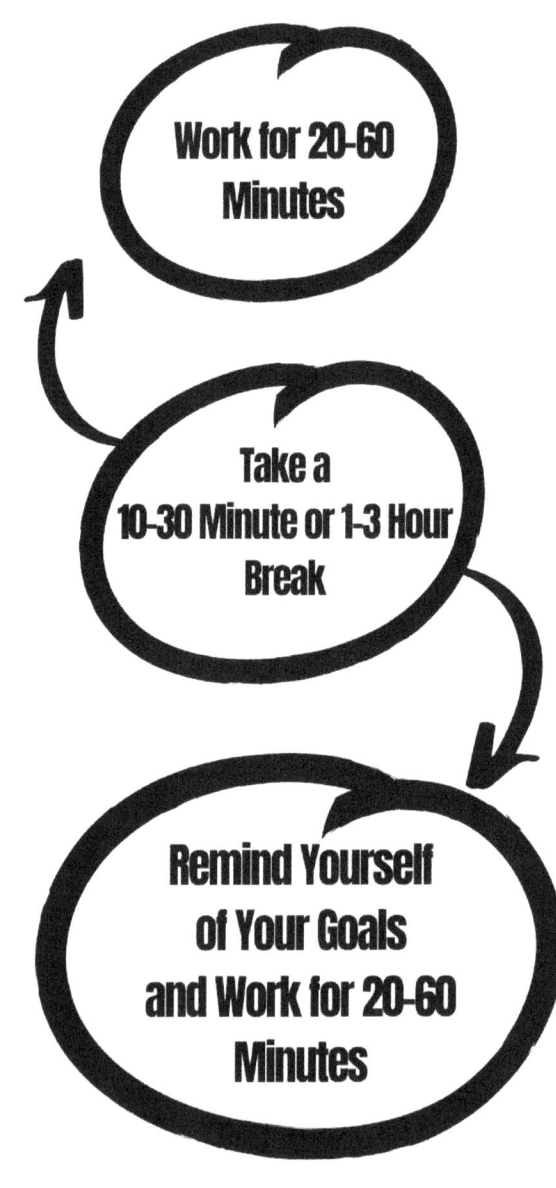

O13

Grow the capacity for healing by connecting with inner child through creative play and exploration

extra thinking space

Grow focus by creating a dedicated space for creative reflection, free from distractions and clutter, where one can fully immerse in the process

Make a List to Self-Monitor Off-Task Impulses

Grow resilience through creative expression, finding solace and strength in the transformative power of art and imagination

extra thinking space

Grow the ability to focus by practicing mindfulness techniques during creative reflection

Create a Self-Compassion List to Give Yourself Grace

- ☐ _____
- ☐ _____
- ☐ _____
- ☐ _____
- ☐ _____
- ☐ _____
- ☐ _____
- ☐ _____
- ☐ _____
- ☐ _____
- ☐ _____
- ☐ _____

Grow the capacity for healing by connecting with your creative, playful, and explorer energy

extra thinking space

Grow ideas by nurturing them with curiosity and exploration

Set 2 Goals and Try 2 Rounds of Using the Timelapse Feature on a Video Camera to Record Yourself and Monitor Your Productivity

Grow consistency by establishing daily routines that support your goals

extra thinking space

Grow ideas by seeking inspiration
from diverse sources and experiences

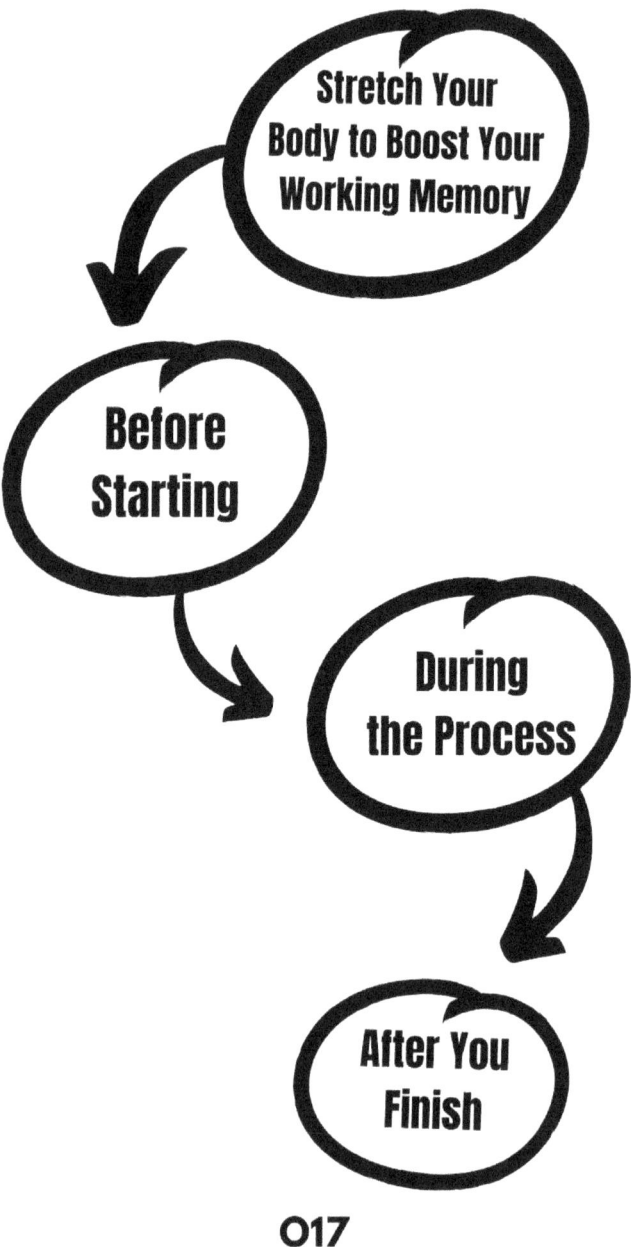

Grow consistency by holding yourself accountable to your commitments

extra thinking space

G.R.O.W. Productivity Guide

G.R.O.W. Productivity Guide

WHEN FINISHED, CREATE

After-productivity strategies to encourage reflective practice, restoration, and play.

Grow success by learning from setbacks and adapting your approach accordingly

Rest
Interactive Progress Journal
Mixed-Medium Vlog
Passion Project
Long Walk in Nature
Long Drive No Destination
Swim or Ride a Bike
Play a Sport
Nature Watching
Visit a Museum or Garden
Color
Paint
Draw
Binge a TV Show
Bake

W1

Grow new ideas by engaging in
brainstorming sessions and creative exercises

extra thinking space

Grow success by celebrating small victories along the way to your ultimate goal

Create a tree of your goals. Add goals as branches of the tree.

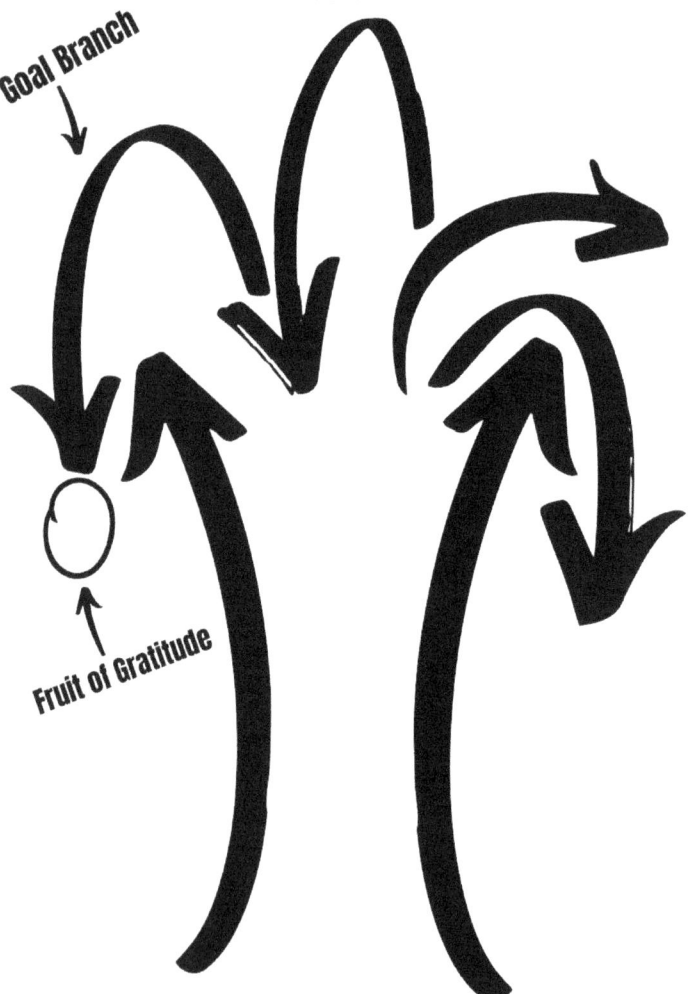

Goal Branch

Fruit of Gratitude

After completion of a task, add a fruit of gratitude to goal-branch worked toward.

W2

Grow ideas by collaborating with others
and embracing different perspectives

extra thinking space

Grow consistency by developing habits
that support your long-term vision

Each time you finish a task, add 1 word to the focus wheel to describe how you _feel_:

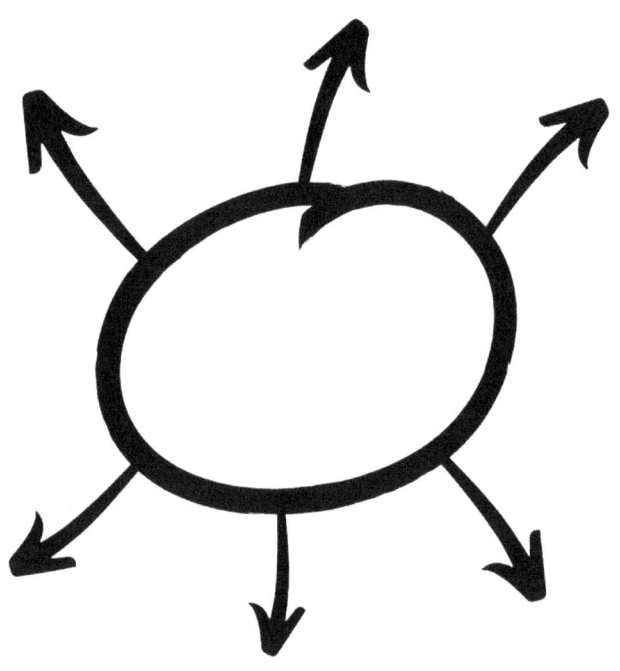

Analyze the trend you find after completing the focus wheel and add 1 final word in the middle to summarize. Make art of the words!

W3

Grow success by maintaining a positive mindset and believing in your abilities

extra thinking space

Grow ideas by experimenting with new techniques and approaches

Make your own dream catcher using items to metaphorically represent the dreams you caught by powering through your productivity session.

Start a capsule of your dream catchers by making one each time you finish your task. Hang them all in your work area as a reminder of your purpose.

W4

Grow consistency by overcoming obstacles
and persevering through challenges

extra thinking space

Grow success by setting realistic milestones and tracking progress

Each time you finish a task, add 1 word to the focus wheel to _define_ your success:

Analyze the trend you find after filling the wheel and make art of the words!

W5

Grow ideas by seeking feedback from peers and mentors to refine concepts

extra thinking space

Grow success by staying flexible and adapting to changing circumstances

List 4 areas you have been able to grow in since you started being more productive

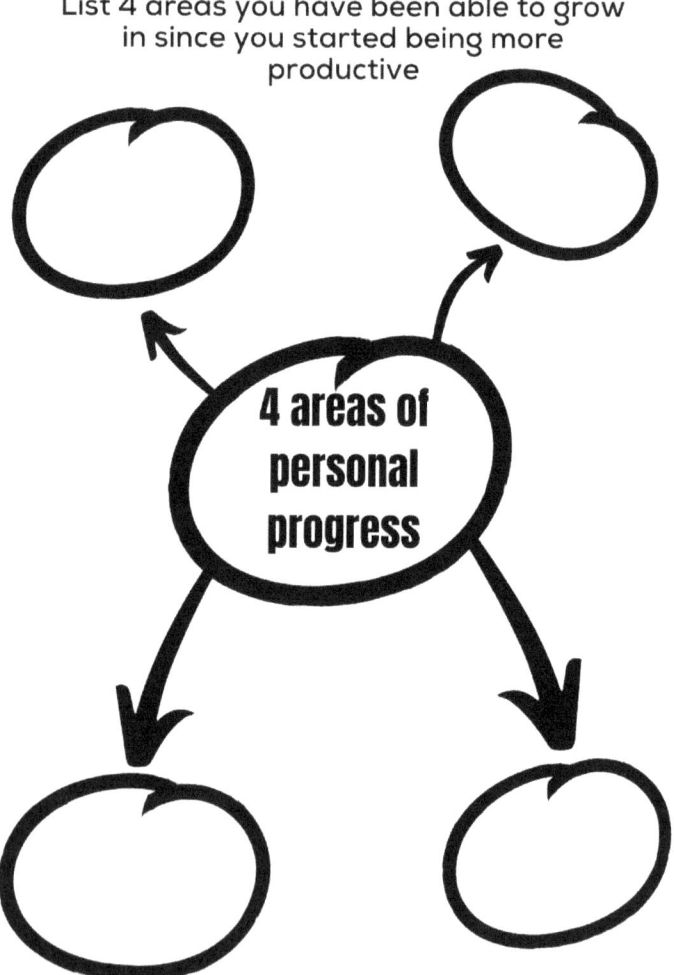

Create a visual that allows you to map your progress points after you complete a task, in order to see how you are evolving as you learn.

Grow ideas by journaling and capturing thoughts regularly

extra thinking space

Grow consistency by reviewing goals regularly and adjusting plans as needed

How can you *measure* your success without grades or outside validation?

Create a visual that allows you to measure your success by your own standards.

W7

Grow success by focusing on the process rather than solely on the outcome

extra thinking space

Grow ideas by immersing yourself in
environments that stimulate creativity

Who were you before you started?
Who are you now that you have made
progress toward completing your goals?

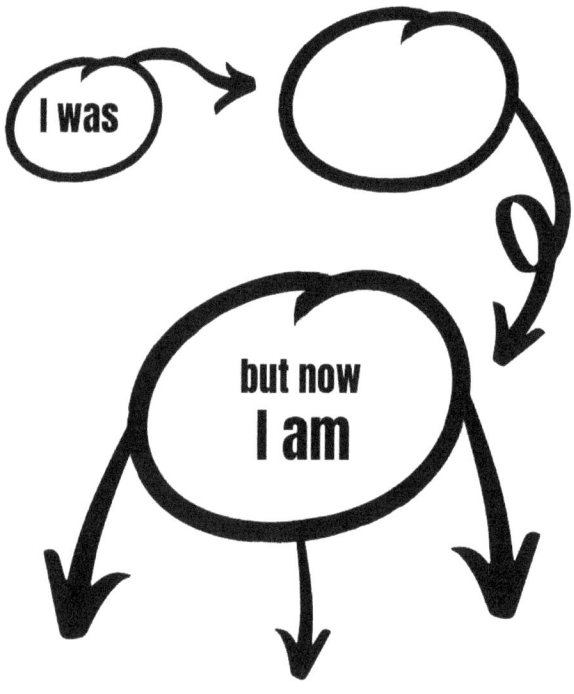

Journal or create self-portraits showing
who you see yourself as.

W8

Grow consistency by practicing self-discipline and resisting distractions

extra thinking space

Grow consistency by establishing accountability systems to keep yourself on track

Make a list of what you needed to shed and what you still may need to shed as you progress beyond procrastination.

Go for a walk and collect a rock for everything you listed.

Find a body of water or field of dirt to sink or bury all of the rocks you collected, as a symbol of letting go of what no longer serves you.

Grow ideas by exploring interdisciplinary connections and intersections

extra thinking space

Grow consistency by setting realistic goals and breaking them down into actionable steps

First list, then, draw how you see yourself reaching your goals

As I reach my goals,
I see myself as

Create a capsule of your drawings to show your evolution as you completed your tasks and grew your productivity.

W10

Grow consistency by practicing patience
and persistence in pursuit of goals

extra thinking space

Grow success by cultivating a growth mindset and embracing lifelong learning

Rename yourself when you are in your productive flow. Look up the meaning of this name and create a collage of the words or symbols that help you to visualize the most productive you.

Be sure to develop a healthy balance between the new named you and your sense of true self.

W11

Grow ideas by actively seeking out inspiration from a variety of sources

extra thinking space

Grow success by visualizing goals
and envisioning achieving them

Choose items from around your house to make a picture frame.

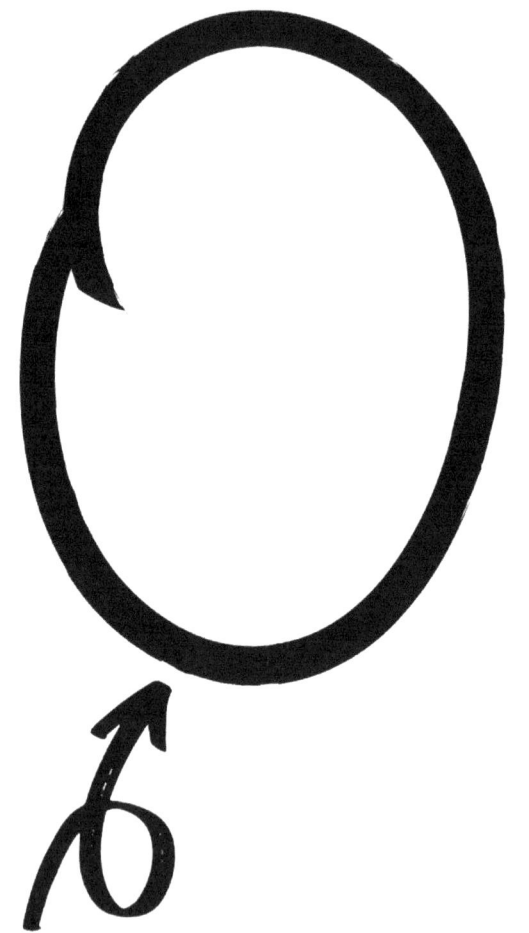

Inside of the frame, add colors, words, photos, or make a new picture that allows you to display your growth.

W12

Grow ideas by challenging assumptions
and questioning the status quo

extra thinking space

Grow consistency by establishing habits that support physical and mental well-being

What resonates with your senses?

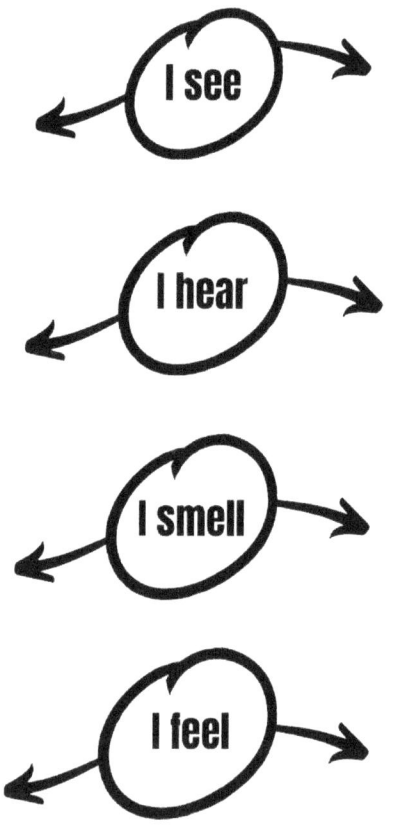

Try this in nature. Use your senses to create a visual you can hang and visuallze when you're in your work-flow.

W13

Grow ideas by reflecting on past experiences and extracting lessons that inform future endeavors

extra thinking space

Grow reflections by engaging in
introspection and self-examination

Create a focus wheel of all of the stories
in your mind:

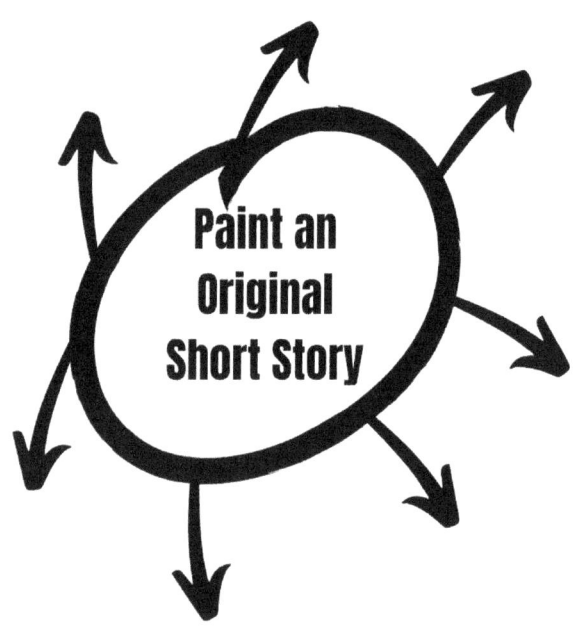

Choose 1 story to start from the list.
Paint it out every time you finish a
productivity session.

Grow transformation by embracing change as a catalyst for growth and evolution

extra thinking space

Grow success by setting ambitious yet achievable goals and pursuing them with determination

Pick up any painting or drawing tools and begin freestylng patterns and dots with colors, shapes, and lines.

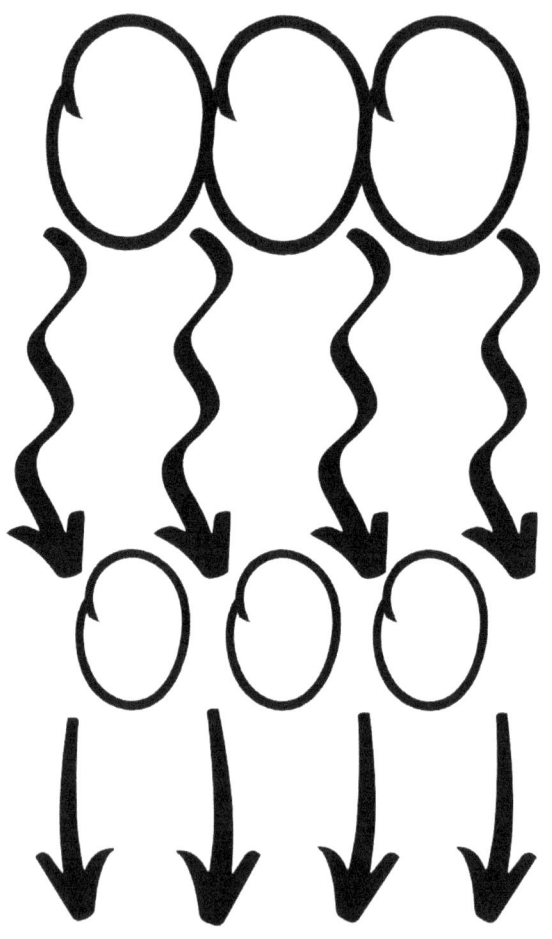

Let your freestyle pattern be a symbol that reflects the different aspect of your progress toward your goals.

W15

Grow transformation by challenging limiting beliefs and embracing new possibilities

extra thinking space

Grow transformation by fostering a
mindset of resilience and adaptability

Create 3-6 layers of doodles by painting or drawing lines or shapes, after you finish a task. With each layer, try to fill in blank spaces.

There is no need to try to make sense of your doodles. Just enjoy the pleasure of guilt free play on canvas.

Grow success by celebrating progress
and milestones along the journey

extra thinking space

Grow transformation by cultivating habits that support personal development and growth

Create a list of all of the small-scale creative projects you ever wanted to try:

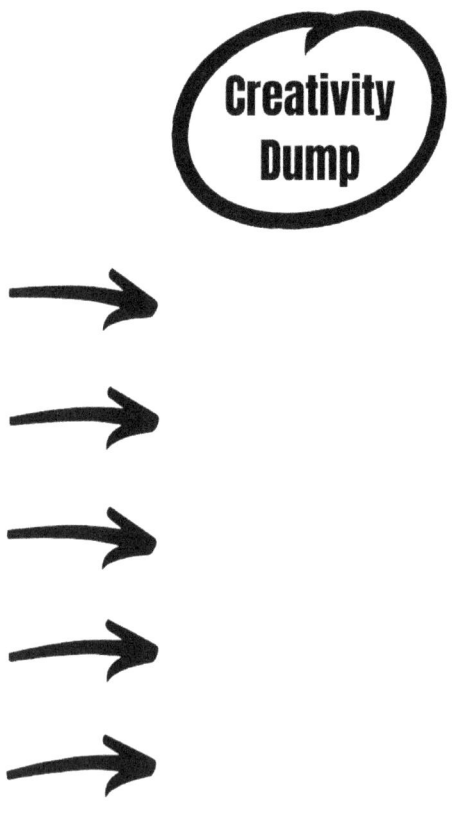

Choose 1 project to start from the list. Work on it every time you finish a productivity session.

Grow success by aligning actions with values and priorities

extra thinking space

G.R.O.W. Productivity Guide

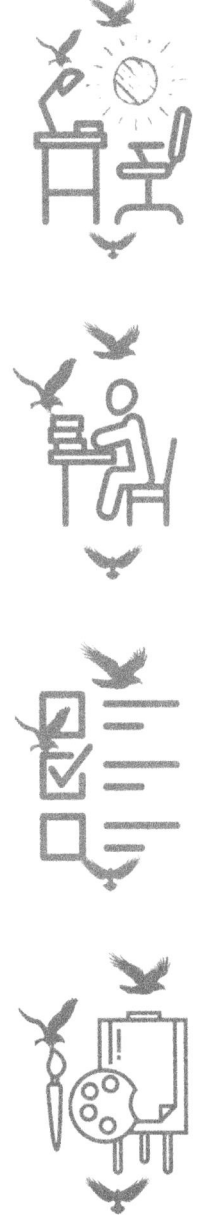

How to Use the Blank Pages

G: **get clear & confident**
USE THIS SPACE TO JOURNAL BEFORE STARTING YOUR WORK

R: **read & refocus**
JOT DOWN YOUR THOUGHTS, NEW LEARNING, AND TRACK READING GOAL PROGRESS

O: **one task at a time**
ORGANIZE, PLAN, AND KEEP NOTES AS YOU EXECUTE

W: **when finished, create**
USE THIS SPACE TO ARTFULLY REFLECT AND EXPRESS

INDEX

Abundance

G8

Academic Boredom

R13

Alternatives

O10

Ambiance

R1

Anchor Chart

R14

Anthology

Introduction

Attention

G5   G7   G15   R1–17   O1–17   W1

Balance

W11

G.R.O.W. Productivity Guide

Best Practices

Introduction

Bitesize Goal

O3

Blank

W16

Blog

R17   W1   W14

Boundaries

G14

Brain-Break

O9

Break

R4   O5   W1

Calendar

R2   O4

G.R.O.W. Productivity Guide

Canvas

EXTRA THINKING SPACE   BLANK WORKSPACE   JOURNAL

Celebration

G12

Chaos

G13

Checklist

O2   O6   O7

Choice

O10

Clear

G3   G4   G6   G7   G10   O5   O12

Collage

W11

Color

W12   G1

G.R.O.W. Productivity Guide

Commit

O4

Confident

G1   G17   W8   W10

Creative

G1   G9

Creative Barriers

INTRODUCTION

Creativity Dump

W17

Daydreaming

R11

Deep Breaths

R4   O5

Distraction

R7   R5   R8   R10   R12   R3   O6   O11   O14

G.R.O.W. Productivity Guide

Doodle

W16

Dots

W16

Draw

W10   W15

Dream Catcher

W4

Ease

G9

Emotional Awareness

O12

Energy

G14

Engagement

G5   R5   R10   R16   O7   O8   O10   O11   O13   O14   O16

G.R.O.W. Productivity Guide

Envisioning

G12   R15

Executive Function

R2   O1–O17

Flexibility

O10

Flow

O6   O11

Focus Wheel

W3

Foldable

R14

Freestyle

W15   W16

Goal

G3   O3

G.R.O.W. Productivity Guide

Grace

O15

Graph

R12

Graphic Organizer

G1-16

Gratitude

W2

Growth

W6

Guilt-Free

R1

Hydrate

R1

Impulse Control

O14

G.R.O.W. Productivity Guide

Independent Task

G10

Intention

G6

Interactive Personal Journal

R14   W1

Intrinsic

INTRODUCTION

Let Go

W9

Lumbar Pillow

R1

Maintain

G13

Meditate

G17   R1

G.R.O.W. Productivity Guide

Mental Noises

R7–9

Metacognition

O1 O2 O12 O14 O16 W5 W6 W8 W12 W13

Metaphor

W3 W4 W8 W9 W10 W11 W12 W13

Mindfulness

G17

Monitor

R5 R8 R11 R12 06 07

Motivation

G4

New You

W11

Note Catcher

R13 R14

G.R.O.W. Productivity Guide

Nutritious

G17

Optimism

G11

Organize

R2   O4   O5

Outcome

R15   R17   O3

Pacing

O6   O7

Page Goal

R2

Paint

W15

Passion Project

G4   W1

G.R.O.W. Productivity Guide

Patterns
W15

Peace
G13

Persistence
O11

Personal Connections
G4

Planning
R2   O4   O7

Play
W1

Power-Through
R10   O11   O13

Preparation
O1   O5

G.R.O.W. Productivity Guide

Priority

G16

Procrastination

W9

Produce

G8   G9

Productive

R1

Progress

R5   O12   W6

Prompt

ALL

Purpose

G7

Reading Goal

R2

G.R.O.W. Productivity Guide

Reels

R10

Reflect

W12

Reflective Practice

W12

Refocus

R1-17

Research-Based

ALL

Restart

R4

Restoration

W1-17

Rounds

O5

G.R.O.W. Productivity Guide

Schedule

R2   O4   O6   O7

Scrapbook

R14

Self-Accountability

G3   G16   R5   R10   R11   R12   O4   O6   O7   W6

Self-Compassion

G17   O15

Self-Determination

G2   R10   O2   O6   O7   W6   W7   W8   W9

Self-Portrait

W8

Share

R17

Shed

W9

G.R.O.W. Productivity Guide

Social Thinking

R17

Space

R4   O5

Space-out

R4

Stamina

R12

Sticky-note

R15

Stillness

G10

Stories

W14

Strategy

ALL

G.R.O.W. Productivity Guide

Stretch-break

R6

Success

W7

Sustained Attention

R1-14   O1-17

Symbol

W11   W15

Tally

R5   R8

Time

R12   O6   O8   O13

Timelapse

R10   O16

Time Management

O4   O6   O7

G.R.O.W. Productivity Guide

Timer

O8

Validation

INTRODUCTION

Video Learning

G15

Vision Board

R15

Visions

G12   R15

Visualize

R1   W11   W13

Vlog

R10

Work-flow

W13

G.R.O.W. Productivity Guide

Working-Memory

O1   O17

Work Out

G17   W1

Workspace

R11   R14   R15

References Organized by Tool

1. After Productivity Activities

Pijpker, R., Kerksieck, P., Tušl, M., De Bloom, J., Brauchli, R., & Bauer, G. F. (2022). The role of off-job crafting in burnout prevention during COVID-19 crisis: a longitudinal study. *International Journal of Environmental Research and Public Health*, 19(4), 2146. https://doi.org/10.3390/ijerph19042146

2. Art as Self-Motivation

Elbrecht, C. (2019). *Healing trauma with guided drawing: a sensorimotor art therapy approach to bilateral body mapping*. North Atlantic Books.

Isis, P. D., Bush, J., Siegel, C. A., & Ventura, Y. (2010). Empowering students through creativity: art therapy in Miami-Dade county public schools. *Art Therapy*, 27(2), 56-61. https://doi.org/10.1080/07421656.2010.10129712

3. Before Productivity Activities

Fiord, N. A. (2003) *Overcoming procrastination: practice the now habit and guilt free play*. MJF Books.

Orbé-Austin, L. & Orbé-Austin, R. (2020) *Own your greatness: overcome impostor syndrome, beat self-doubt, and succeed in life*. Ulysses Press.

Church, M. & Ritchhart, R. (2003) *Making thinking visible: how to promote engagement, understanding, and independence for all learners*. Jossey-Bass.

Ahmed, S. K. (2003) *Being the change: lessons and strategies to teach social comprehension*. Heinemann.

Amen, D. G. (2021) *Your brain is always listening: tame the hidden dragons that control your happiness, habits, and hang-ups*. Tyndale Refresh.

4. Body Movement

Bretland, R. J., & Thorsteinsson, E. B. (2015). Reducing workplace burnout: The relative benefits of cardiovascular and resistance exercise. *PeerJ*, 3, e891. https://doi.org/10.7717/peerj.891

Munro, M. (2018). Principles for embodied learning approaches. *South African Theatre Journal*. 31(1), 5–14. https://doi.org/10.1080/10137548.2017.1404435

Rosales-Ricardo, Y., & Ferreira, J. P. (2022). Effects of physical exercise on burnout syndrome in university students. *MEDICC Review*, 24, 36-39. https://doi.org/10.37757/MR2022.V24.N1.7

Wolf, M. R., & Rosenstock, J. B. (2017). Inadequate sleep and exercise associated with burnout and depression among medical students. *Academic Psychiatry*, 41(2), 174-179. https://doi.org/10.1007/s40596-016-0526-y

5. Creating Boundaries

Fiord, N. A. (2003) *Overcoming procrastination: practice the now habit and guilt free play*. MJF Books.

Glover-Tawwab, N. (2021) *The set boundaries workbook: practical exercises for understanding your needs and setting healthy limits*. TarcherPerigee.

Orbé-Austin, L. & Orbé-Austin, R. (2020) *Own your greatness: overcome impostor syndrome, beat self-doubt, and succeed in life*. Ulysses Press.

G.R.O.W. Productivity Guide

6 Creative Reflection Questions

Mathisen, G. E., & Bronnick, K. S. (2009). Creative self-efficacy: an intervention study. *International Journal of Educational Research*, 48(1), 21-29.

Maciej Karwowski (Editor), James C. Kaufman (1997). *The creative self: effect of beliefs, self-efficacy, mindset, and identity (explorations in creativity research) 1st edition.* Academic Press.

Beck, H. (2019) *Scatterbrain: how the mind's mistakes make humans creative, innovative, and successful.* Greystone.

7 Creativity Theory

Glaveanu, V. P., Hanchett Hanson, M., Baer, J., Barbot, B., Clapp, E. P., Corazza, G. E., ... & Montuori, A. (2019). Advancing creativity theory and research: A socio-cultural manifesto. *The Journal of Creative Behavior*, 1-5. https://doi.org/10.1002/jocb.395

8 During Productivity Activities

Hadwin, A. F., Davis, S. K., Bakhtiar, A., & Winne, P. H. (2019). Academic challenges as opportunities to learn to self-regulate learning. *In H. Askell-Williams & J. Orrell (Eds.), Problem Solving for Teaching and Learning.* Routledge https://doi.org/10.4324/9780429400902-4

Miyatsu, T., Nguyen, K., & McDaniel, M. A. (2018). Five popular study strategies: Their pitfalls and optimal implementations. *Perspectives on Psychological Science*, 13(3), 390–407. https://doi.org/10.1177/1745691617710510

Muijs, D., & Bokhove, C. (2020). *Metacognition and self-regulation: evidence review.* Education Endowment Foundation.

Pèrez-Álvarez, R., Maldonado-Mahauad, J., & Pèrez-Sanagustín, M. (2018). Tools to support self-regulated learning in online environments: literature review. *In European Conference on Technology Enhanced Learning.* Springer, Cham.

Serravallo, J. (2015). The reading strategies book: your everything guide to developing skilled readers. Portsmouth, NH: Heinemann.

van de Pol, J., van Loon, M., van Gog, T., Braumann, S., & de Bruin, A. (2020). Mapping and drawing to improve students' and teachers' monitoring and regulation of students' learning from text: current findings and future directions. *Educ Psychol Rev* 32, 951–977 (2020). https://doi.org/10.1007/s10648-020-09560-y

9 Elaboration & Transfer

Brown, P.C. (2014). *Make it stick: the science of successful learning.* Harvard University Press.

Eraut, M. (2009). 2.1 Transfer of knowledge between education and workplace settings. In H. Daniels, H. Lauder, & J. Porter (Eds.), *Knowledge, values and educational policy: a critical perspective* (pp. 53–73). Routledge.

10 Engagement

Csikszentmihalyi, M. (2008). Flow: The Psychology of Optimal Experience World. Grand Central Publishing.

Newport, C. (2017). Deep Work: Rules for Focused Success in a Distracted World. Grand Central Publishing.

Stobaugh, R. (2019). *Fifty strategies to boost cognitive engagement: creating a thinking culture in the classroom - 50 teaching strategies to support cognitive development.* Solution Tree Press

11 Emotions

Arguedas, M., Daradoumis, T., & Xhafa, F. (2016). *Analyzing how emotion awareness influences students' motivation, engagement, self-regulation and learning outcome. Educational Technology & Society,* 19(2), 87–103. http://www.jstor.org/stable/jeductechsoci.19.2.87

Trenton, N. (2021) *Stop overthinking: 23 techniques to relieve stress, stop negative spirals, declutter your mind, and focus on the present.* NCTS, Inc.

12 Executive Function

Executive function strategies blog posts. ThePathway2Success.com. Retrieved September 2022

Johnson, J., & Reid, R. (2011). Overcoming executive function deficits with students with ADHD. *Theory into Practice*, 50(1), 61–67. https://doi.org/10.1080/00405841.2010.534942

Mitsea, E. & Drigas, A. (2019). A journey into the metacognitive learning strategies. *International Journal of Online and Biomedical Engineering* (iJOE), 15(14), pp. 4–20. https://doi.org/10.3991/ijoe.v15i14.11379

Otero, T. M., Barker, L. A., & Naglieri, J. A. (2014). Executive function treatment and intervention in schools. *Applied Neuropsychology: Child*, 3(3), 205–214. https://doi.org/10.1080/21622965.2014.897903

13 Future-Time Perspective

Bembenutty, H., & Karabenick, S. A. (2004). Inherent association between academic delay of gratification, future time perspective, and self-regulated learning. *Educational Psychology Review* 16, 35–57. https://doi.org/10.1023/B:EDPR.0000012344.34008.5c

Rosenzweig, E. Q., Hulleman, C. S., Barron, K. E., Kosovich, J. J., Priniski, S. J., & Wigfield, A. (2019). Promises and pitfalls of adapting utility value interventions for online math courses. *Grantee Submission*, 87(2), 332–352 https://doi.org/10.1080/00220973.2018.1496059

Schuitema, J., Peetsma, T., & van der Veen, I. (2014). Enhancing student motivation: a longitudinal intervention study based on future time perspective theory. *Journal of Educational Research*, 107(6), 467–481. http://dx.doi.org/10.1080/00220671.2013.836467

Tsai, M.-Y. (2015). The Relationships among Imagination, Future Imagination Tendency, and Future Time Perspective of Junior High School Students. *Universal Journal of Educational Research*, 3(3), 229–236. https://doi.org/10.13189/ujer.2015.030309

14 Goal-Setting

Boot, N., Nevicka, B., & Baas, M. (2020). Creativity in ADHD: goal-directed motivation and domain specificity. *Journal of Attention Disorders*, 24(13), 1857–1866. https://doi.org/10.1177/1087054717727352

Muis, K. R., Ranellucci, J., Franco, G. M., & Crippen, K. J. (2013). The interactive effects of personal achievement goals and performance feedback in an undergraduate science class. *Journal of Experimental Education*, 81(4), 556–578. https://doi.org/10.1080/00220973.2012.738257

Wehmeyer, M., Hughes, C., Agran, M., Garner, N., & Yeager, D. (2003). Student-directed learning strategies to promote the progress of students with intellectual disability in inclusive classrooms. *Int. J. Inclusive Education*, 7(4), 415-428. https://doi.org/10.1080/1360311032000110963

15 Gratitude

Bono, G., & Sender, J. T. (2018). How gratitude connects humans to the best in themselves and in others. *Research in Human Development*, 15(3-4), 224-237. https://doi.org/10.1080/15427609.2018.1499350

16 Internal Distractions

Schleider, J. L., Mullarkey, M. C., & Dobias, M. L. (2021) *The growth mindset workbook for teens: say yes to challenges, deal with difficult emotions, and reach your full potential.* Instant Help.

Helmstetter, S. (2014) *The Power of neuroplasticity*. Park Avenue Press.

Responsive Classroom (2016) *Responsive classroom refocus and recharge! 50 brain breaks for middle schoolers.* Center for Responsive Schools, Inc.

17 Mind Mapping

Knight, K. (2012) *Mind mapping: improve memory, concentration, communication, organization, creativity, and time management*. Mind Lil

18 Motivation

Nagashibaevna, Y. K. (2019). Students' lack of interest: how to motivate them? *Universal Journal of Educational Research,* 7(3), 797–802. https://doi.org/10.1111/1467-9604.12340

Mendler, A. N. (2021) *Motivating students who don't care: proven strategies to engage all learners, second edition.* Solution Tree Press

19 Outdoors Activities

Barnes, M. R., Donahue, M. L., Keeler, B. L., Shorb, C. M., Mohtadi, T. Z., & Shelby, L. J. (2019). Characterizing nature and participant experience in studies of nature exposure for positive mental health: An integrative review. *Frontiers in Psychology,* 9, 2617. https://doi.org/10.3389/fpsyg.2018.02617

Meredith, G. R., Rakow, D. A., Eldermire, E. R., Madsen, C. G., Shelley, S. P., & Sachs, N. A. (2020). Minimum time dose in nature to positively impact the mental health of college-aged students, and how to measure it: A scoping review. *Frontiers in Psychology,* 2942. https://doi.org/10.3389/fpsyg.2019.02942

20 Procrastination

Fiord, N. A. (2003) *Overcoming procrastination: practice the now habit and guilt free play.* MJF Books.

Fishbach, A. (2022) *Get it done: surprising lessons from the science of motivation.* Little Brown Spark

Lieberman, C. (2019). *Why you procrastinate (it has nothing to do with self-control).* New York Times, 25.

21 Productive Environment

Lisa, S. N., & Dwiyanti, E. (2022). Literature study of work accompaniment music to effect on employee productivity in several companies. *Journal of Public Health Research and Community Health Development,* 5(2), 73-79. http://dx.doi.org/10.20473/jphrecode.v5i2.26528

McLoughlin, C., & Lee, M. J. W. (2010). Personalised and Self Regulated Learning in the Web 2.0 Era: International Exemplars of Innovative Pedagogy Using Social Software. *Australasian Journal of Educational Technology,* 26(1), 28–43. https://doi.org/10.14742/ajet.1100

22 Progress Tracker

Ayobi, A., Sonne, T., Marshall, P., & Cox, A. L. (2018). Flexible and mindful self-tracking: design implications from paper bullet journals. *In Proceedings of the 2018 CHI Conference on Human Factors in Computing Systems* (pp. 1-14). https://doi.org/10.1145/3173574.3173602

Fiord, N. A. (2003) *Overcoming procrastination: practice the now habit and guilt free play.* MJF Books.

Fishbach, A. (2022) *Get it done: surprising lessons from the science of motivation.* Little Brown Spark

Marwan, S., Shabrina, P., Milliken, A., Menezes, I., Catete, V., Price, T. W., & Barnes, T. (2021). Promoting students' progress-monitoring behavior during block-based programming. *In 21st Koli Calling International Conference on Computing Education Research* (pp. 1-10). https://doi.org/10.1145/3488042.3488064

23 Reflective Practice

Carroll, R. (2018). *The bullet journal method: track the past, order the present, design the future.* New York, New York: Portfolio/Penguin.

Mezirow, J. (1998). On critical reflection. *Adult Education Quarterly,* 48(3), 185-198.

Rogers, S. (1997) *Motivation & learning: a teacher's guide to building excitement for learning & igniting the drive for quality.* Peak Learning Systems

G.R.O.W. Productivity Guide

24 Rest

Wolf, M. R., & Rosenstock, J. B. (2017). Inadequate sleep and exercise associated with burnout and depression among medical students. *Academic Psychiatry*, 41(2), 174-179 https://doi.org/10.1007/s40596-016-0526-y

25 Self-Actualization

Hill, C. L., & Updegraff, J. A. (2012). Mindfulness and its relationship to emotional regulation. *Emotion*, 12(1), 81–90. https://doi.org/10.1037/a0026355

Lanaj, K., Foulk, T. A., & Erez, A. (2019). Energizing leaders via self-reflection: A within-person field experiment. *Journal of Applied Psychology*, 104(1), 1. https://doi.org/10.1037/apl0000350

26 Self-Determination

Ryan, R. M. & Deci, E. L. (2018) *Self-determination theory: basic psychological needs in motivation, development, and wellness*. The Guilford Press.

27 Self-Regulatory Learning

Bjork, R. A., Dunlosky, J., & Kornell, N. (2013). Self-regulated learning: beliefs, techniques, and illusions. *Annual Review of Psychology*, 64(1), 417–444. https://doi.org/10.1146/annurev-psych-113011-143823

Cho, M.-H., & Heron, M. L. (2015). Self-regulated learning: the role of motivation, emotion, and use of learning strategies in students' learning experiences in a self-paced online mathematics course. *Distance Education*, 36(1), 80–99. https://doi.org/10.1080/01587919.2015.1019963

Cleary, T. J., & Platten, P. (2013). Examining the correspondence between self-regulated learning and academic achievement: a case study analysis. *Education Research International*, https://doi.org/10.1155/2013/272560

Reddy, L. A., Cleary, T. J., Alperin, A., & Verdesco, A. (2018). A critical review of self-regulated learning interventions for children with attention-deficit hyperactivity disorder. *Psychology in the Schools*, 55(6), 609–628. https://doi.org/10.1002/pits.22142

Wehmeyer, M., Hughes, C., Agran, M., Garner, N., & Yeager, D. (2003). Student-directed learning strategies to promote the progress of students with intellectual disability in inclusive classrooms. *Int. J. Inclusive Education*, 7(4), 415-428. https://doi.org/10.1080/1360311032000110963

28 Storytelling as Therapy

Ricks, L., Kitchens, S., Goodrich, T., & Hancock, E. (2014). My story: The use of narrative therapy in individual and group counseling. *Journal of Creativity in Mental Health*, 9(1), 99-110. https://doi.org/10.1080/15401383.2013.870947

29 Summarizing & Generation

Brown, P.C. (2014). *Make it stick: the science of successful learning*. Harvard University Press.

Hao, N., Ku, Y., Liu, M., Hu, Y., Bodner, M., Grabner, R. H., & Fink, A. (2016). Reflection enhances creativity: Beneficial effects of idea evaluation on idea generation. *Brain and Cognition*, 103, 30–37. https://doi.org/10.1016/j.bandc.2016.01.005

Roediger, H. L., III, & Butler, A. C. (2010). The critical role of retrieval practice in long-term retention. *Trends in Cognitive Science*, 15(1), 20–27. https://doi.org/10.1016/j.tics.2010.09.003

30 Visualization

Waalkes, P. L., Gonzalez, L. M., & Brunson, C. N. (2019). Vision boards and adolescent career counseling: A culturally responsive approach. *Journal of Creativity in Mental Health*, 14(2), 205-216.

GROW WITH US

Dear Creative,

Many share the desire to maximize productivity and personal empowerment. We hope the G.R.O.W. formula helps you flourish.

This guide was curated by Growcery Garden, a bookshop and creative community dedicated to uplifting the imaginations of diverse creators, leaders, artists, builders, writers, educators, scholars, and healers. Our name reflects our belief in growth and progress. We aim to support creatives in their endeavors, whether they create for themselves or for the communities they serve.

We offer productivity support through self-regulatory learning strategies, collaborative co-working sessions, playlists, and self-paced courses. We invite you to attend our virtual workshops or live group sessions during the year. To register visit growcerygarden.org.

Valenciá and Fabian D. Bell
Author/Designer and Publisher/Producer

Growcery Garden
BOOKSHOP & CREATIVE COMMUNITY
ROOTED IN PRODUCTIVITY & PROSPERITY